"All over this nation, God is stirring the hearts of men to rise up and enter into their God-given destiny. Lou Turner's lifelong passion is to see men enter into their divine purpose in life. 'Living Life God's Way,' of which this book is a part, is born out of this passion. Throughout this Bible study series, Turner opens up God's Word to help you discover HIS plan for your success in your life, family, and work. If you are ready to get off the treadmill, to begin to enjoy God's fullness in your life and make a significant contribution to the world around you, I recommend that you dive into this life-transforming Bible study."

Hal H. Sacks, D.Min., *BridgeBuilders International Leadership Network*

"It seems North American culture is rapidly moving toward what the Bible calls 'everyone doing what is right in his own mind' (Judges 21:25). The prophet Isaiah declared, 'Woe to those who call evil, good, and good, evil' (Isaiah 5:20). This Bible study series will challenge every man in the 21st century as 'iron sharpens iron'! The Q&As at the end of each chapter really personalize the teaching."

Dennis Conner, *Co-Founder/President, Called to Serve Prayer-Coaching Ministry*

"I have known Lou Turner for over twenty years. Lou loves Jesus and has built his life on the Word of God. Lou's Bible study series, 'Living Life God's Way,' is full of biblical truth that has been tested and can be applied by disciples of Jesus in practical ways. These books will help you grow in your faith and gain confidence and competence, which will increase your fruitfulness in Christ.

Mark Buckley, *Founding Pastor of Living Streams Church*

Living Life God's Way

A Man and His Children

Lou Turner

A Man and His Children
First Edition, 2020
Copyright © 2020 by Lou Turner

A Man and His Children is part of the Living Life God's Way Series by Lou Turner.

All rights reserved. No part of this publication may be reproduced, stored in a retrieval system, or transmitted in any form by any means—electronic, mechanical, photocopy, recording, or otherwise—except for brief quotations in critical reviews or articles, without the prior permission of the publisher, except as provided by U.S. copyright law.

Unless otherwise marked, Scriptures are taken from the ESV® Bible (The Holy Bible, English Standard Version®) copyright © 2001 by Crossway Bibles, a publishing ministry of Good News Publishers. ESV Text Edition: 2016. The ESV® text has been reproduced in cooperation with and by permission of Good News Publishers. Unauthorized reproduction of this publication is prohibited. All rights reserved.

Scripture quotations marked (NIV) are taken from the Holy Bible, New International Version®, NIV®. Copyright © 1973, 1978, 1984, 2011 by Biblica, Inc.® Used by permission of Zondervan. All rights reserved

Scriptures marked NKJV are taken from the New King James Version®. Copyright © 1982 by Thomas Nelson. Used by permission. All rights reserved.

Scripture quotations marked (TLB) are taken from The Living Bible, copyright © 1971 by Tyndale House Foundation. Used by permission of Tyndale House Publishers, Carol Stream, Illinois 60188. All rights reserved.

Some of the anecdotal illustrations in this book are true to life and are included with the permission of the persons involved. All other illustrations are composites of real situations, and any resemblance to people living or dead is coincidental.

ISBN: 978-1-7331186-3-7

To order additional books:
www.amazon.com
www.hislifeinus.com

Editorial and Book Packaging: Inspira Literary Solutions, Gig Harbor, WA
Book Design: PerfecType, Nashville, TN
Cover Design: MTWdesign, Dickson, TN
Printed in the USA by Ingram Spark

He will be like a tree firmly planted by streams of water,
Which yields its fruit in its season
And its leaf does not wither;
And in whatever he does, he prospers.

Psalm 1:3

TABLE OF CONTENTS

Preface   ix

How to Use this Book   xi

Introduction   xiii

1. The Importance of a Father   1

2. Loving Your Children   15

3. Teaching Your Children   29

4. Leading Your Children   39

5. Passing on Godly Character   53

A Final Word   65

About the Author   67

PREFACE

We live in a world that has largely forgotten what manhood is about. In the Western world, men are usually portrayed on television as buffoons who are out of touch and must rely on their wives to straighten them out. These characters are portrayed as silly, insensitive, lacking common sense, and when they do speak, they are generally wrong. They are usually portrayed as either ridiculously weak or overly macho. They are not able to commit to a long-term relationship and are often guilty of mistreating women. Positive role models are hard to find in the media.

However, the Bible teaches a different type of manhood, the authentic one. Men are to be leaders, loving their wives and children, excelling in their work, and standing for truth. They are to be men of wisdom, knowledge, having godly character and seeking after God and His direction. They are to be exhibiting godly leadership at church, in the community, and in business, and to be a light to those around them. They are to be men of compassion and love, as well as courageous and bold when needed.

Men go astray from these ideals, including Christian men, due to improper convictions or beliefs about life. They have received these from various sources: well-meaning family and friends, the media, and the culture around them—a world system that promotes the tearing down of God's biblical truths.

PREFACE

But without proper biblical foundation, we will all go astray.

That's why I wrote these books, containing insights, observations, and biblical truths distilled over the course of my decades of life and ministry. Each section is designed to be a stand-alone section for study and consideration. I hope this series, *Living Life God's Way*, will be used to disciple men in biblical truths for life. Whether you use it for yourself, with a group, or to mentor or disciple someone else, my hope is that it will be a blessing to you and encourage you to seek God and grow in Him.

HOW TO USE THIS BOOK

What does it mean to be a "good" husband and father?
How do I live out the Christian life at work?
What does God want from me—and how am I supposed to find that out?

These were questions that plagued me as a young man—questions, I learned, that are at the front of many men's minds at various times in their lives. For me, these questions began my quest to seek God and discover the answers I needed. My discoveries, over the years of my life, led to this series of booklets, *Living Life God's Way*. While I do not suggest that I have discovered all of the answers, my desire is to share what I have learned and hope it will be helpful for you. This series discusses 13 topics that every man must deal with, regardless of his work, calling, profession, or circumstances. It is difficult to know how to live the Christian life without understanding what God says about these areas of life.

These topics are:

1. Seeking and Finding God
2. Who You Are in Christ
3. A Man's Work and Ministry
4. A Man and Authority
5. A Man and His Wife

HOW TO USE THIS BOOK

6. A Man and His Children
7. Getting Guidance from God
8. Overcoming Strongholds
9. A Man and Money
10. Repentance, Forgiveness, and Restitution
11. Being a Leader
12. A Man and Sex
13. The Test of Pride

You can use these books to study on your own, in a small group, or with a larger group of men. Each topic or booklet is a stand-alone study, and a person can begin with any one he chooses. They are different lengths and can be adapted to various settings—home, church, or community—all topics that are pertinent to today.

Explore what the Bible says about these important and critical parts of life. The encouragement is to read these with an open heart, asking God to reveal His truth to you in each of these areas. Pray that His Spirit will show you His truth, so that you may live in it and enjoy all God has for you. I pray that you experience the blessing and presence of God in your life as you draw closer to Him and become more aware of His leading in every area of your life.

INTRODUCTION TO A MAN AND HIS CHILDREN

The purpose of this study is to lay down basic principles about a man's relationship with his children.

Raising children is one of the greatest challenges in life, and one of the greatest fulfillments and pleasures of life. This responsibility requires large amounts of time, patience, love, concern, money, creativity, flexibility, consistency, courage, and conviction. We must have the ability and willingness to grow individually as new demands are made on us as fathers. No experience in life will try us, grow us, change us, reward us, and fulfill us more than parenting.

God created and ordained the family unit, just as He did marriage. From the beginning, His plan was that the man and woman He created would be able to reproduce and have children. While some couples are not able to have their own children, or chose not to, most couples are able to have children.

My own children are now grown and I have grandchildren. I love my family, my children, and my grandchildren. I cannot imagine life without them. My family is a blessing from God and any "stretching times" I went through while they were growing up were well worth it.

Learning from those who have already walked this path successfully, and getting their counsel, can save a lot of heartache and bring great joy. Growing in our parenting skills gives insight into God's nature and purpose, the ability to love and forgive, and to become more like Christ in our character. It's a great adventure and offers rewards like nothing else.

Chapter 1

THE IMPORTANCE OF A FATHER

> *"Father involvement has a unique impact on children's outcomes, including cognitive development, achievement, math and reading scores, as well as behavioral problems."*
> —W. Jean Yeung, Sociologist,
> University of Pennsylvania

Joan and I married when we were both twenty, and she became pregnant seven months later. We did not plan this; it somehow just happened! We now had to learn how to be good parents while we were still learning how to be good spouses. By the time I was twenty-six, I was a father of three. Joan and I both felt strongly that she should be available to care for our three young children full time, so I was very motivated to work and provide for my family.

Like all fathers, I had to learn to balance my busy life and priorities. I wanted to be there for my children and be involved in their lives, because I knew that fathers are important.

While many may lead you to believe that a father is just another potential caregiver for children, research shows that the presence of a loving father has a great impact on the family and the future of their children. Let's look at some statistics:

Fathers teach their children to care for others. A twenty-six-year study published by the American Psychological Association found that children whose fathers were involved in their lives were more likely, as adults, to be sensitive to the needs of others. In addition, researchers found that the qualities of generosity and thoughtfulness were more prevalent in adults whose fathers had been very involved in their lives.

Children with involved fathers are more confident. Fathers tend to challenge their children to try difficult things and take measured risks. Since we gain confidence by actually trying something difficult and discovering we can do it, children with involved fathers tend to have more confidence. Infants with involved fathers are more confident and more likely to explore the world around them with enthusiasm. Fathers have a more active play style and are slower to help their children through frustrating situations, which creates greater problem-solving capacity and confidence in both boys and girls. In a review of studies on father involvement and child well-being, 82 percent of studies found "significant associations between positive father involvement and offspring well being."

Children with involved fathers tend to have increased vocabulary. As children spend more time with their fathers, they are likely to have larger and more complex vocabularies. Mothers tend to talk on a child's level, which can give immediate benefit. However, fathers tend to speak with their children more like they speak to adults. Dad's instructions to their children tend to be longer, and to give their children the opportunity to hear more words and learn how words fit together to convey a thought. An article in *Developmental Psychology* found that well-fathered preschool boys and girls had increased verbal skills compared to those with absent or overbearing fathers.

A father's presence helps prevent crime and acting-out behavior. Studies show you are not likely to find boys in gangs who have loving, involved fathers. Insecure boys are often attracted to gangs to give them identity and a perceived way to act out their manhood. Boys with loving fathers learn that they are important, loved, and valued. They don't feel the need to "force" their manhood but grow into it more naturally.

Girls with loving fathers are less likely to give in to the pressures of being sexually active. They are more confident, already feeling that they are loved and important to their father, the most important male in their life until they meet their future husband.

Fathers promote better treatment of women. Because a loving father shows his love to his wife and children, his children learn how a man should treat others. Because of his loving and caring involvement, his daughters feel valued and his sons learn to treat women with respect and value them.

Research including 90 different cultures reported that in societies with significant paternal involvement in routine child care, women are more included in public decisions and allowed to have a more significant role in society. Why? Because loving fathers value their daughters and wives and want to see them succeed in what they do. Thus there is a greater respect for women in general.

A father's love helps promote school readiness, behavior, and performance. Children with involved fathers tend to show up for school with more of the character qualities needed for learning. They are more patient, curious, and confident. They are better able to remain in their seats, wait patiently for their teachers, and maintain interest in their work.

Higher levels of self-control in children with involved fathers was also associated with many other healthy qualities, such as improved general life skills, self-esteem, and higher social skills. Positive fatherhood also caused their children to have lower levels of disruptive behavior, depression, and telling lies. The children tend to be happier and willing to try new things. Positive father care is associated with more pro-social and positive moral behavior overall in boys and girls.

Higher education levels. Research from the University of Pennsylvania found that children who feel closeness and warmth with their father are twice as likely to enter college, 75 percent less likely to have a child in their teen years, 80 percent less likely to be incarcerated, and half as likely to show various signs of depression. The likelihood that a young male will engage in criminal activity doubles if he is raised without a father and triples if he lives in a neighborhood with a high concentration of fatherless families.

We have discussed the positive ways fathers affect their children. I want to share some facts with you about what happens to children when they don't have a father active in their lives. I realize all children technically have fathers or they wouldn't be here. But many children do not have fathers involved in their lives. So by "without fathers," I mean there is no father actively involved in their life.

- Since 1968, the number of children without fathers has doubled to over 18 million. Fathers are having children out of wedlock and are not fathering them.
- Currently, the majority of children born to women under 30 are born out of wedlock. These children have no father in their life.

THE IMPORTANCE OF A FATHER

- Less than half of adults today grew up without both a mother and father involved in their lives.
- Of teens with behavioral problems, 85% have no dad in their lives. Of adolescents in drug and alcohol treatment centers, 70% have no dad.
- Of homeless and runaway children, 90% have no father.
- Children with no father are 90% more likely to drop out of school.
- Men who grow up without fathers are 200% more likely to be in prison.
- Children with no fathers are 200% more likely to be neglected or abused.
- Women comprise 81% of single parents.
- Children without a father are 500% more likely to live in poverty.
- Men are more likely to be idle or non-productive in life if they have no father involved in their life.
- Of rapists, 80% had no involved father in their life.
- If a father becomes a Christian, the family is over 70% more likely to become Christians as well.
- If a father attends church, the children are 70% more likely to attend church as adults.*

Fathers, don't let anyone make you feel you are not important. You are very important to your family, even if you feel inadequate at times. You make a great and vital contribution to your marriage and your children's lives. God has entrusted you with a special responsibility.

Obviously, we are not talking about mean, cruel, or abusive fathers. Those types of fathers can do great damage to their children. Because of a father's importance to his children, an abusive

---

* Statistics cited are are from various sources, including Focus on the Family.

or cruel father can harm his children emotionally and mentally. In sharing the positive impact a father can make, we are talking about fathers who love their children and try to father them. There are no perfect fathers, but fathers who try to father and love their children have a great influence over them and can be a positive force for good.

Malachi 4:5-6 states, *"Behold, I will send you Elijah the prophet before the coming of the great and dreadful day of the Lord. And he will turn the hearts of the fathers to the children, and the hearts of the children to their fathers, lest I come and strike the earth with a curse."* When men have revival in their hearts, their love of their children grows and they become more involved in their lives. Children in turn respond to their fathers and their hearts are turned toward them. The result is a stronger family, and children who grow up much more stable and much more likely to serve the Lord. Men, you should never doubt your influence in the family—especially when you take an active role.

Children Are a Father's Trust from God

God tells us that children are a blessing to a father. In turn, a father is to be a blessing to his children.

> *Behold, children are a heritage [blessing] from the LORD, the fruit of the womb is His reward. Like arrows in the hand of a warrior, so are the children of one's youth. Happy is the man who has his quiver full of them; they shall not be ashamed, but shall speak with their enemies in the gate. (Psalm 127:3-5)*

A father plays a vital role in his children's lives. Obviously, a mother cannot be a father, nor can a father be a mother; both are needed as each brings a unique blend of gifts and attributes to the family. God made men and women, and made them to be different. The importance of the father's role in raising children should never be minimized. As we have shown, good fathers have great, positive impact on their children.

Looking back, would I have done some things differently as I raised my children? Of course. I always tried to do the right thing, but at times, I made mistakes or did the wrong thing. But children forgive you when they know you love them and value them. Being a father stretched me, at times stressed me, matured me, and changed me. I had to learn how to love and how to father. I am a different man because of this; thank God!

Our Children Need to Know They Are Important to Us

Many dads reading this will likely relate to this process of maturing as a father. I think of a story I heard about Tommy, who was five years old and playing in his first soccer game. His dad had gone to most of the practices to watch him and give him encouragement and tips about how to excel. Tommy's dad had been an athlete and he wanted his son to be one, too—a great one.

However, Tommy did not excel in his first game. In fact, he didn't do very well at all. His dad was disappointed. He loved his son, but he had certain expectations that were very important to him. One was for his son to excel in everything in which he became involved. Tommy had not lived up to his dad's expectations, and his dad was upset.

When he and his dad arrived at home, his dad began to vent over his disappointment in Tommy's performance. Not only was he upset, he spoke openly about it within Tommy's hearing. The young boy wanted his father's approval and was keenly aware that he had failed. Rather than build up his son and encourage him, assuring him that he loved him, Tommy's dad let his son know that he had failed. That's a tough thing for a five-year-old to live up to—or forget.

A father's personal goals for his children can vary from being extremely high to none at all. Dads can be overzealous and overbearing. They can also be uncaring, detached, or even abandon their children. What does the Bible tell us about being a father? Does it give us guidance? Yes, it does.

The Bible teaches us that children are a gift from God. This puts us in a position of trust from God. We are their earthly fathers, but God is their heavenly father. We are responsible for bringing them up in a manner that pleases Him. Our goal is not to make children in our image, but in God's image—that is, in His desired character qualities as described by the Bible. As fathers, we should teach our children these godly or biblical character traits. One of the roles of a father is to be a loving teacher to our children.

Teach Your Children God's Ways

Moses gave the Israelites a special commission to teach their children:

> *Hear, O Israel: The LORD our God, the LORD is one! You shall love the LORD your God with all your heart, with all your souls, and with all your might.*
>
> *And these words which I command you today shall be in your heart; you shall teach them diligently to your children, and shall talk of them when you sit in your house, when you walk by the way, and when you lie down, and when you rise up. (Deuteronomy 6:4-5)*

This great challenge is one that Jesus modeled for us. As He went through life with His disciples, He taught and trained them about God's ways. As we go through life with our children, we should be teaching and talking to them about God's ways and biblical character.

This doesn't have to be a classroom setting. We are to teach or discuss this when we "sit in [our] house," when we spend time with our children at home. Part of that time is talking to them about character and life lessons as situations arise. However, we should also set aside time to communicate biblical values to our children.

The passage also says we should teach our children when we **"walk by the way."** This means as we go about life's activities. Life brings abundant opportunities to teach and discuss important things with our children.

Teaching our children when they **"lie down,"** or at bedtime, is another great time to communicate. **"Rising up,"** or at breakfast, may be difficult due to schedules, but mealtime is a great time to talk to our children and have quality time with them.

The verse says we are to teach them **"diligently."** This does not mean we are overbearing or constantly hovering over our children to correct their every thought and action. It does mean we work with and teach them consistently, not sporadically. Of course, all of this means we are spending regular time with our children. Our motivation is one of love and caring for them. This is the type of relationship Jesus modeled for us.

A word about teaching. This does not mean we are always in teaching mode. No one likes to be taught constantly. Talking to them about important things is a way to teach without them feeling like we always have to be teaching. They need to be fathered, loved, and spent time with on a regular basis. Yes, we should teach them, but it should be done relationally—not making them feel like they are always in a classroom. We can use humor, stories, projects with object lessons, and just discuss life and their circumstances. The chances for input are endless.

Jesus Modeled God's Fathering

Jesus was a great example. Jesus loved people. He accepted them and made them feel valued. He reached out to the outcasts of society—the rejected and lowly, the sick and the poor—and He lifted them up. He spent time with them. He taught them. He healed them and gave them hope. He defended them against the hypocritical religious leaders of the day.

He taught them to love each other, to forgive, to value their relationships with others and with their heavenly Father. He told them they did not have to live up to the law in order for God to accept and love them. He loved them just as they were, with all of their faults and shortcomings.

The religious leaders taught them they had to be perfect and live up to the complex religious laws of the day in order to measure up. Jesus taught them that God greatly valued them in spite of their transgressions, and they should seek God for relationship with Him.

They needed to discover who God really was, not who the religious system said He was. They had lost sight of a loving God who cared for them and had come up with a religious system with rules and regulations that no one could live up to, including the religious leaders, though they wanted everyone to believe they could.

As Jesus walked with His disciples, He demonstrated love for them, He lived out godly character, He taught them, trained them, allowed them to make mistakes, corrected them, and challenged them. He built them up; He did not tear them down.

Who would have picked the people He did to change the world? He chose fishermen, a tax collector—men others would have passed over. But Jesus looked into their lives and saw their potential. As fathers, we need to look into our children's lives and see their potential. More important, we should ask God to show us how *He* views them and to reveal their potential to us. Our children need our encouragement to become what God has for them.

God Knows Our Children Better than We Do

God knows our children intimately. He knows how they are gifted, their talents, their aptitudes, their abilities, and His plan for their life. We should pray and seek God to lead our children in His path for them. *It may be different than our plan for them.*

The Lord will give us insight into our children and how we should teach and train them, love them, and lead them. As we seek Him, He will reveal these things to us. We will not understand His entire plan for their lives, as He will reveal that to them as they grow up and seek Him. But, He *will* give us insight into how to parent them.

This is the type of fathering our children need. Children need fathers who will love them, spend time with them, and make them feel accepted and valued. God wants fathers who will teach their children the truth, proper values, and to seek after Him. He wants fathers to love and accept their children.

Our children will remember many things as they grow up, and after they are grown. One of the main things they will remember is whether they felt loved and accepted by their dads. Their relationship with their fathers will have an impact on them for good or for harm.

As men, we must determine to have a positive impact on our children by our unconditional love and acceptance. Even if we feel we blew it during those growing up years, it is never too late to start loving and encouraging our children, and being a positive force in their lives.

We Need to Grow into Parenting

We all bring pre-conceived ideas into marriage and parenting. Some are healthy and right on, some are idealistic, and some are damaging and hurtful. More important are the things we bring into parenting that are in our hearts and souls. We can bring positive or negative attitudes, joy and love, or wounds and hurts; we can bring ideals, goals, and good intentions. We can also bring negative things like anger, a lack of patience, and demanding and hurtful attitudes.

Regardless of all we bring, by seeking God, praying over our parenting, and learning to practice good parenting behaviors and skills, we can become great parents. We also can learn to be great grandparents.

Remember, there are no perfect parents, but great parenting is possible. We will make mistakes and may experience heartache. However, we can learn and grow in our abilities to parent. Parenting can bring joy, pleasure, a sense of fulfillment, happiness, and love in our relationships with our children.

Because Joan and I had children so young, we had to mature and finish growing up together while we also learned to be parents. It was a challenge. We made a lot of mistakes. But we loved our children and each other, we sought God for help and wisdom, and we found some great help and counsel from older couples in our church.

I am not sure how it would have turned out without God's help, as well as the help of others. We were always sincere, but sometimes we were sincerely wrong. But we took one step at a time, learned to be patient with each other, learned to pray a lot, and somehow have a great son and two great daughters whom we enjoy today.

Were there challenges? Yes. Was it worth it? Yes. Was I always the best father? No. Did I make mistakes? Yes. But I didn't give up, and as I prayed over my children, God gave me help as I needed it. Today I am thankful for my children, their spouses, and my grandchildren. They truly help complete my life.

QUESTIONS FOR REFLECTION AND DISCUSSION

1. Do you realize the importance men have in fathering children? Write out in your own words how you believe fathers can affect their children.

2. What do you want your children to remember about you as a father?

3. Do you think your children feel accepted and valued by you? How do you know this?

4. Do you take time to teach and train your children? To talk to them about life? How do you do this?

_____

_____

_____

_____

TAKE A KNEE

Let's kneel before the Lord and pray. If you are physically unable to kneel, then kneel to God in your heart. *"Father, help me to realize how important my presence is to my children. Show me how I affect them, both positively and negatively. Teach me how to be a more positive influence on them in every area and how to bless their lives. I ask your Holy Spirit to teach me how to be the best father I can be.*

I realize I have many responsibilities, but I want to make my children the proper priority they should be. Teach me and train me in this area. I ask for wisdom and insight. Help me to humble myself to get input from others as I need to. Thank you for my children."

Chapter 2

LOVING YOUR CHILDREN

First and foremost, love your children.
Be loving and kind in all you do.

Every father should memorize 1 Corinthians 13. It is only 13 verses long, yet memorizing and prayerfully thinking on these verses is life-changing. Take up the challenge and commit it to memory. You can do it! It will help teach you what love is, and what it is not.

Learning to love is one of the greatest challenges in life. Loving people, especially our families, is of utmost importance to God. When a Jewish lawyer asked Jesus what the greatest commandment was, Jesus replied,

> *You shall love the Lord your God with all your heart, with all your soul, and with all your mind. This is the first and*

greatest commandment. And the second is like it; you shall love your neighbor as yourself. On these two commandments hang all the Law and Prophets. (Matthew 22:37-40)

This encounter is also mentioned in Mark 12:28-31 and Luke 10:25-27. This message was important and God wanted us to get it; that's why it is repeated three times! So what did Jesus say? He said to love God and love others. These are the greatest commandments! I think it deserves to be said again. The greatest commandments are "love God" and "love others." All of the other laws and commandments revolve around these two things. So, all of the laws of Exodus, Leviticus, Numbers, and Deuteronomy can all be summed up by "love God" and "love others." All of the laws in those books, as long and extensive as they are, revolved around those two things. So, what are we supposed to do? Learn to love God and learn to love others. Sometimes we need to have things repeated a number of times before we get the message.

Loving others includes our children. In fact, they are at the top of the list, just under our wife, just after God.

Part of loving our children is praying for them. We cover our relationship with them with prayer. Prayer releases God's Spirit to be active in the things we are praying about.

For men, when we are married and have children, we begin by *learning* to love our families. We do this through spending time with them, being patient with them, letting them know we love and value them, and being involved in their lives. We can also demonstrate our love for our children by praying for them. **Covering our relationship with our children with prayer, and seeking God for wisdom, causes Him to become active in our relationship with our children.**

We will make mistakes as fathers; however, if our children feel loved and valued, they will continue to feel secure in their relationships with us. We need to tell our children we love them. But even more important, we need to show them we love them.

Our Children Need to Know They Are Loved and Valued

People know we love them by our words, our actions, and our attitudes toward them. First John 3:18 says, "My little children, let us not love in word or in tongue, but in deed and in truth."

> *Children know we love them by our words, our actions, and our attitudes.*

We cannot love them only in words; they also need actions. And if we have more than one child, our children need to know that we love them individually, not just as part of a group.

Some men, due to past hurts they have experienced, may have hardened their hearts to try to protect themselves. They may not know how to love their children or others. Many confuse love with sex. For others, the type of love they may have experienced has left a warped concept of love in them. They may not know how to love their children or how to allow their children to love them. They may not have experienced a dad who knew how to love them. It wasn't modeled for them and so they need to learn how to love their children.

Learning to love our children takes practice and prayer. We all need to ask God to show us how to love. We need to ask Him to put His love, a supernatural love, in our hearts first for Him, then for our family, including our wife and children. For many, this also means learning to love the family we came from, including our siblings.

I think God gets excited when we ask Him to do this and teach us how to love. After all, He demonstrated His love for us by sending His one and only son to die for us when we didn't deserve it. That's love!

The need for love is a human thing. We all need it and our children need it. We all need to be loved and appreciated. Our children need to be shown affection. Hugging them, kissing them appropriately, and telling them you love them and value them have a great impact on our children. This is especially important for our children so they grow up with an experience of being loved we may not have had.

Discipline, teaching, and training from a father without love can result in deep resentment, anger, rebellion, fear, and possibly even hatred. A lack of patience or harshness will breed anger, rejection, and insecurity in our children. When children know they are loved and valued, they are far more open to their father in all areas of parenting. The Bible states in Ephesians 6:4, *"Fathers, do not exasperate (provoke or use anger) your children; instead bring them up in the training and instruction of the Lord."*

This message is repeated in Colossians 3:21: *"Fathers, do not embitter (discourage them with anger) your children, or they will become discouraged."*

In James 1:20, it states, *"Man's anger does not bring about the righteous life that God desires."*

Proverbs 15:1 also says, *"A gentle answer turns away wrath, but a harsh word stirs up anger."*

Anger stirs up more anger. If you are an angry parent, your children will most likely be angry at you and others. Anger does not accomplish righteousness. Love, instruction and prayer do.

If you are a father who struggles with feeling loved or has trouble loving others, you should begin to pray about this area. Ask God to reveal His love for you and ask Him to supernaturally love your wife and children through you.

This is important! If you have a problem loving your family, being patient with them, or a problem with anger, you need help. Ask God to help you. Begin to pray over these areas daily

and ask God to change your heart and renew your mind in these areas. Get counsel if needed. But attack these areas with prayer. Don't put it off. Your family needs you to love them.

This is a powerful prayer, and one that God delights to answer. As you continue to pray about this area, God will begin to reveal His love to you and teach you how to love. You will change. He will give you greater love for your wife and children. Pray over this area daily for thirty days and see what God does!

Our Children Need to Be Cared For and Safe

Our children also need fathers who will provide for them and protect them. Children do not have to feel like their parents are rich to feel cared for and safe. In fact, a family may have meager means and the children can be happy and feel secure.

> *When children have their needs met*
> *and know their father loves them,*
> *values them, and will protect them,*
> *they will feel cared for and safe.*

Beyond provision, a father needs to foster an atmosphere or family culture in which his children can thrive. The family culture is the "atmosphere" in the home. Does your family culture make your children feel safe, accepted, valued, and secure in their relationship with you? Can they approach you to discuss important topics and get input that is both biblically based and love motivated? Is the home a place of love, joy, meaningful discussion, fun, and healthy relationships?

As a father, you need to take the lead in establishing this culture or atmosphere. Obviously, a mother also has a great influence on family culture and on her children, as she should. When the father and mother work together, with the father taking the lead, the results are greater than with just one parent trying to raise the children. (I am not trying to minimize the importance of the mother in the family, but am seeking to emphasize the importance of the father.)

Our Children Need to Know They Were Born with the Sex God Wanted Them to Have

Transgenderism is a lie of Satan. Children are born either male or female, and that is what they are intended to be. The current practices of confusing our children and trying to transform them into the opposite sex is ungodly. As a father, you need to reinforce to them their gender and speak out against transgenderism. They need to know the truth.

Our Children Need to Experience Affection

Part of loving is showing affection; everyone needs affection. We all need to be hugged, loved, and affirmed. Again, some fathers, because of their past, may shun affection or not know how to give it. Many adults were not shown affection as children; thus they did not learn both to receive and give it. Possibly they had harsh or abusive parents and the area of affection shut down or never developed. Regardless, our children both need to be told they are loved and to be shown they are loved by acts of affection such as hugging or kissing on the cheek.

In some cultures, as boys become young men, it is more appropriate for mothers to kiss them on the cheek than it is for fathers. In other cultures, it is acceptable for the fathers to kiss their sons and show appropriate affection that way. But regardless, fathers can hug them, affirm them, and show affection to them in other ways.

Men, if we have trouble demonstrating love by showing affection, we need to make a conscious decision to begin to show affection to our children. Of course, I am not speaking of inappropriate affection. God will help us in this area if we ask Him.

If this is an area of struggle or difficulty for you, be aware that God wants to show you that He loves you. The more we feel loved, the easier and more natural it is to show love to others. **As you learn to receive God's love, you will have greater love to show to others.**

God desires to show His love and affection toward us, and for us to show love and affection to our families. He greatly desires to heal any hurts or wounds in our lives so we can receive His love for us and in turn, be a channel for Him to love others through us. He desires for us to be able to both receive and give love and affection.

Our Children Need to Have Fun with Us

God gave us a sense of humor and the ability to laugh and have fun. We should enjoy our children. Laugh with them, have fun with them, and teach them the joy of family. The father should take the lead in setting aside family time for fun and enjoyment. If there is no fun or joy in the home, our children will look elsewhere for this important part of life.

These times can be a great exercise in creativity. You and your wife can team up and find ways to have great fun and meaningful time with your children.

Time Well Spent

In order to experience our love, care, protection, affection, and fun, our children need our time. God does not want us to neglect the gift He has given us in the form of our children. We must spend time with them in order for them to know we love them. Also, time with our children gives us opportunities to teach and train them. Likewise, we must spend time with them in order to give them wise counsel.

Spending time with our children helps us be involved in their lives, and get to know them. What natural gifts and talents do they have? What are their interests? What are their spiritual motivations? As they get older, how does God want to lead them? How can we understand our children unless we spend time with them? Knowing our children in these ways unfolds over time as we are with them and pray for them.

Seek God's priorities. Being involved with our children does not mean we abandon all other pursuits. Some parents build their entire lives around their children's activities—often to a fault. Perhaps it is because they feel no purpose for their own lives apart from their work. Parents have their own gifts, callings, ministries, and activities in which God wants them involved.

Practicing balance in this area is very important. We do not want to abandon the activities, callings, or ministries God has for us. But we also cannot abandon our children. We do not want to neglect the things God has for us outside of our families. But we also do not want to neglect our families. A father who neglects his family is violating his God-given priorities. His neglect will cause problems in the family and the individual lives of his children.

A man should view his ministry to be to his family first, and then to others. If a man cannot minister to his own family, how can he teach other men to minister to their families? First Timothy

3:5 says, *"If anyone does not know how to manage his own family, how can he take care of God's church?"*

Emergencies and difficult circumstances may arise which might take large amounts of time on a short-term basis. However, in our life's priorities, our families must take a very high place. Time with our family is where we are to learn to love, teach, train, and develop godly character and insight.

A Christian minister told me that when he attended Bible school he was taught that he should put "God's work" first and then God would take care of his family. His children grew up without the time and influence they needed and there were many problems. They made some wrong and devastating decisions and their lives suffered. Later in his life, he admitted the instruction he received was wrong. He should have put his family first and not neglected them. He neglected his relationship with his children and there were some very difficult things they all had to deal with.

If you think you may not be in balance here, pray and ask God for wisdom or seek godly counsel. Remember, God promises to give wisdom to all who ask for it (James 1:5).

Girls and Boys. One thing that needs to be addressed is something that should be obvious—boys and girls are different! You might say, "Yes, I know that." However, as fathers we must realize that while all children have needs in common, they also have needs that are different.

Boys and girls need to be loved unconditionally but differently. Just as each child is different and needs to be understood and treated according to his or her uniqueness, so boys and girls are different in general and need to be treated accordingly. Often, fathers spend time with their sons and daughters in the same ways. But at times, boys and girls have specialized needs.

Daughters need their fathers' attention and time. If a girl does not receive love and attention from her father when she is young, as she gets older she will seek it from other males (possibly not those that are best for her). A girl needs to feel her father loves her, accepts her, and values her. A father should plan and spend time with his daughter. "Dating" her by taking her out to do things just with her is especially important. During these times, communication will open and understanding and insight will grow. She will feel valued and loved. She will not forget these times.

When my daughters were young, I often tucked them in at night and talked to them. I tried to be involved in all of their school activities and spend time with them. As a family, we played games, played hide and seek, had squirt gun fights, and I read Bible stories to them each Thursday night. They got busier as they got older, and it seemed to get more difficult to spend quality time with them. My wife filled this role well and was very involved with my daughters. Looking back, I feel like my daughters needed more individual time with me in their pre-teen and teen years. Though I can't relive those years for my daughters, I do try to let them know I love them now and how special they are to me. I want them to know they are loved, valued, and have a special place in my heart that only they can occupy.

If there is a bond between a girl and her father, as she gets older, the things that are important to keep the relationship going will be there—namely understanding, communication, trust, and love. The role model a father shows his daughter will have a great influence on her choices of a mate.

Sons also need their fathers' time. Fathers need to spend time with their sons doing "guy stuff." Not every father likes to hunt and fish, but they can find common ground with their sons and spend time with them. It may be sports, building a car engine, woodshop activities making things, going to the lake, or just talking about life. Boys look to their fathers for acceptance; their fathers are role models of manhood and fatherhood. Each man is different, and there is no ideal personality for a father or for a man. God made us with differing talents, abilities, interests, and spiritual gifts. However, some qualities are essential in all fathers and men, including good character and a desire to seek God.

Fathers should model, to the best of their ability, biblical character. Fathers should also, by praying together, demonstrate to their sons that they seek the Lord. A man's character, including honesty, integrity, relationships with others (both male and female), work and work ethics, along with other key topics should be taught and communicated from fathers to sons. Fathers and sons should also share activities or working on projects together. These activities are great bonding times, and great opportunities for fathers to teach their sons.

Spending time with your sons and daughters is important. Praying with them is very important and sets an example of seeking God for direction. In large families, it may be harder to spend individual time, especially the more children you have. But you can carve out time to spend with them, even if it is shorter time with them individually and more time with them in two's or three's or as a group. But you can show them love individually.

They will feel valued as we spend time with them, encourage them, give them positive input, give them responsibilities and praise them for accomplishing tasks.

QUESTIONS FOR REFLECTION AND DISCUSSION

1. How would you describe your family culture—the atmosphere of your home and family?

   _____

   _____

   _____

2. Do you think your children know you love them? How do you show your love to them?

_____
_____
_____

3. Do you show affection to your children? If so, how?

_____
_____
_____

4. Have you ever asked your wife to tell you her opinion of how you father your children? What is her feedback? If you have not asked her, what do you think her feedback would be? (Make sure you ask her.)

_____
_____
_____

5. Do you spend regular uninterrupted time with your children? If so, after reading the above, are there activities you think you should add to your time with your children? If so, what are they?

_____
_____
_____

TAKE A KNEE

Let's pray: *"Father, raising children is challenging. Trying to balance all of my responsibilities is also challenging. I desire to be the father You desire me to be. Give me insight and understanding how to do this. Show me how to spend quality time with my children and how to make them feel loved and valued."*

Chapter 3

Teaching Your Children

The pastor spoke on Sunday morning. He boldly proclaimed, "It is not this church's job, or my job, to be the primary teacher of your children about the things of God. It is the parent's responsibility to teach their children the Bible, teach them about God, and instill biblical values and character in them. I am here to reinforce what you should already be teaching them."

Though a few of the parents were taken back by this bold statement, he was right. The Bible lays the responsibility for instructing our children about the Bible and about their relationship with God with the parents. The Bible specifically says a father is to teach his children.

> *You shall love the Lord your God with all your heart and with all your soul and with all your might. And these words that I command you today shall be on your heart. You shall teach them diligently to your children, and shall talk of*

> them when you sit in your house, and when you walk by the way, and when you lie down, and when you rise. (Deuteronomy 6:5-7)

God laid out a promise in Genesis for fathers who give godly instruction to their children. In speaking about Abraham, God said, *"For I have known him, in order that he may command his children and his household after him, that they keep the way of the Lord, to do righteousness and justice, that the Lord may bring to Abraham what He has spoken to him"* (Genesis 18:19).

Scripture states numerous times that a blessing will come on children whose father teaches them the ways of God. If a father purposes to be an example to his children of living by and keeping God's Word, and in turn teaches his children to do the same, the Bible says God's blessing will come on both the father's home and upon the children.

This is further emphasized in Psalm 103:17-18: *"But the mercy of the LORD is from everlasting to everlasting on those who fear Him, and His righteousness to children's children, to such as keep His covenant, and to those who remember His commandments to do them."*

These are great promises and should motivate all fathers to desire God's blessings on their homes and children. Obviously, parents cannot teach the Bible and instruct their child about biblical things unless they themselves are studying God's Word.

In Proverbs, we read about King Solomon being instructed by his father, King David:

> *My son, hear the instruction of your father, and do not forsake the law of your mother; for they will be graceful ornaments on your head, and chains about your neck. (Proverbs 1:8-9)*

> *When I was my father's son, tender and the only one in the sight of my mother, he also taught me, and said to me; "Let*

your heart retain my words; keep my commands, and live."
(Proverbs 4:3-4)

In the same way, we are to instruct our children. Teaching and instruction must be done with patience and in love, with the goal of developing biblical and sound character in our children's lives. We don't want them to feel like they are in school. But as we discuss life and what is happening with them, and how the Bible says to deal with their situations, they learn and are taught.

As I mentioned earlier, for a number of years I set aside Thursday nights to read to my children. Specifically, I read through books that spoke of character qualities that we should all have. These books spoke about and defined character qualities and included a Bible story and an example in nature to back it up. It was well-illustrated and my children seemed to enjoy it.

I also read books of the lives of missionaries and those who stepped out in faith to accomplish things God had led them to do. I tried to add humor and make it fun. I'm not sure if I always succeeded, but it gave input into their lives and gave us some good family time.

What to Teach

Below are some topics a father should be teaching his children—all of which the Bible addresses directly or indirectly. I realize this is a long list and can be somewhat intimidating, but it can be taken one step at a time.

1. **Who God is.** God's ways, His faithful and loving nature, and a healthy fear (awe and respect) of the Lord (Proverbs 1:7).
2. **Practical work skills.** Teach or encourage your children to develop skills that will help them in life. Find out how they

are gifted or motivated and encourage them to develop their gifts.
3. **Handling money.** Teach children to be responsible, pay their bills or debts on time, not overextend themselves, how to balance a checkbook, and to save money.
4. **Sex.** When they are ready, teach your children that sex is a gift from God to be enjoyed and shared in marriage between a man and woman. Share with them the dangers and consequences of sex outside of marriage.
5. **Dating.** The Bible doesn't mention dating—this is a modern-day custom. A father should give guidelines in this area and not allow TV or Hollywood to teach his children about relationships with the opposite sex and the process of finding a spouse.

    Dating, especially at a young age, is not a healthy activity for teenagers. Putting teenage boys and girls alone for hours at a time is just not wise. Group situations with others you approve of can be much healthier. Don't accept society's norms in this area, but seek God as to what is best for your child. Remember, at sixteen or seventeen, teens are part adult and part child. They still need guidance, direction, and protection from questionable activities. It is a danger to convince yourself that your child is "mature for his/her age" and can handle it. Many "mature for their age" girls have gotten their hearts broken or pregnant. And many "mature for their age" boys have gotten into a lot of trouble they should not have.
6. **Developing godly character.** Teach your children character traits such as honesty, initiative, diligence, perseverance, courage, and humility.
7. **Respect for others.** Teach them respect for other people and a proper respect for others property.

8. **Respect their parents.** It's easier to respect parents that love them. One way to model this is to love your own parents and let your children see that.
9. **Authority.** Teach children to respect authority, to have a serving attitude toward those they work for, to serve them with confidence, and to have positive, healthy attitudes.
10. **Morality.** Teach them God's standard of morality, what is right and wrong and how to conduct themselves. Also teach them God's standard for sexual morality.
11. **Work and a work ethic.** Teach your children to work, take initiative, take pride in their work, and to be thorough and complete tasks.
12. **Prayer and seeking God.** This is the most important thing you can teach your children. Teach them to pray and how to pray. Teach them to set aside time to read their Bible and seek God for direction for their lives. Praying with them and teaching them from the Bible is a great way to model this.
13. **Practical and spiritual gifts.** Help children discover their natural talents and gifts along with their spiritual gifts or motivations, which begin to come out after they accept Christ as their Savior.
14. **Personal relationships.** What is friendship and how should they treat their friends? What does it mean to love others? How do they love others in a practical manner? Teaching kindness and consideration of others are great qualities which God blesses.
15. **Family relationships.** Your children need to learn to get along with and love their siblings. Teach them to respect and love their grandparents and other family members.
16. **Forgiveness.** Teach them to forgive others for wrongs suffered.

17. **Courage and boldness.** Help your children overcome fear and act with courage when appropriate. Teach them what courage and boldness are.
18. **Meekness, humility, compassion, and kindness.** Teach them what these qualities mean and practical ways to live them out.
19. **The authority and validity of the Bible.** God's Word is truth and life to their souls as they read and study it. Help them to develop respect for and a love of the Bible.
20. **Creation versus evolution.** There are lots of good books on this topic, which you and your children can read together. When children grow up and are in high school and college, their faith will be challenged and most instructors will teach evolution as fact. Your children need good teaching in this area to establish biblical foundations to stand on. Scientific discoveries continue to dispute evolution and support creationism. Get some good books on this subject. The Institute on Creation Research has some great books on this.

This list is by no means exhaustive; there are many other important biblical principles and doctrines. Every child needs practical instruction in these and other subjects according to their individual needs.

Don't be discouraged by the list. I realize it can look intimidating and maybe overwhelming. But you don't have to do it all at once. Take it a step at a time. The topics above make it obvious that teaching our children is ongoing. If your children are young, you have a lot of years and many opportunities to talk about these things. And, you don't have to be a college professor to talk about these things and teach them to your children.

I realize we are all busy, but you can take one topic at a time. Study it yourself and then discuss it with your children. Not only will your children grow, so will you!

When and How to Teach

You can't do this without setting aside time to teach and instruct our children regularly so they will be better equipped for life. We are not talking about classroom teaching, but instructing and discussing these things with our children and spending time talking about God's truth as a way of life.

Many might say, "I am not a teacher." Not everyone is a gifted teacher, but all can learn to communicate with their children. You may feel unqualified to teach or train your children on the above topics. However, as you read and study the Bible and other resources that are wise, practical, and in agreement with the Bible, over time you will see these topics covered.

Also, you can pick a topic, do some study on it, and then share what you have learned with your children on their level. In this way, you are continually learning and able to share truth with your children. It's easy to make a list of topics, study yourself, and then teach your children a bit at a time. Obviously, this needs to be done on their level in a way they can understand.

Remember, no one wants to be treated harshly or dealt with in anger. We want our children to blossom, not withdraw. If our children fear us, something is wrong. If we teach and instruct in love, then they will not fear us.

There is ample opportunity to teach your children in daily life. If your children are being mean-spirited toward their siblings, you can teach them to love and forgive, and show them what that means on a practical level. If they are fearful, you can encourage them and share stories from the Bible about courage. If they lack confidence, your love and assurance will make them feel more secure. Tell them of God's love for them and that He values them.

Teaching your children is not a daunting task. Like eating an apple, you take one bite at a time. As situations come up, you respond, encourage, discuss, and teach. As you see a need in your child's life you encourage, discuss, teach, and train. Pray about this and pray for your children. God will show you practical ways to do this. He is faithful. Setting aside time for your family can be fun and rewarding. Don't ever underestimate the influence you have on them!

QUESTIONS FOR REFLECTION AND DISCUSSION

1. Do you spend time teaching your children? If so, what things do you share with them? Please list them below.

   _____
   _____
   _____
   _____

2. Are you setting aside regular weekly time to share with your children the truths of God's Word? If so, how do you do this?

   _____
   _____
   _____
   _____

3. What is a practical way you can pray and seek God about your responsibility of teaching and training your children?

   _____
   _____
   _____
   _____

TAKE A KNEE

Let's pray: *"Father, please show me how to teach and train my children. Show me how to be creative and make it meaningful and relevant to them. Reveal to me the topics I need to cover with them. Help me to be disciplined to set aside the time to accomplish this. I ask Your Holy Spirit to anoint me to do this in love."*

Chapter 4

LEADING YOUR CHILDREN

When Joan and I were married, I wanted to be a good husband and father, but honestly didn't know how. I loved her and our children, but many of my concepts of marriage, relationship, and being a father were lacking. I was fortunate to become part of a church where these things were taught. I was challenged to grow and be the father and husband I needed to be.

With time and effort, as I prayed, sought God, and studied the Bible, I began to change my habits and my thinking and put forth effort at being a better husband and father. Some of my thinking and ways changed dramatically. They needed to. I set aside time with Joan and time with our children.

Every night when I came home from work, I began to take responsibility for some of the things that needed to be done with our children, both to relieve Joan and spend time with the children: getting them baths, tucking them into bed, playing with them. Joan needed some alone and recovery time, and I and my children needed some time together. We were busy, and usually two or three evenings a week were taken with activities and church. But the other evenings I tried to devote myself to Joan and my children.

Both the Old Testament and the New Testament stress the need for fathers to take leadership in the home and to teach and train their children. Obviously the mother will also have great influence in teaching and training them, as she should. But the father cannot neglect his responsibility with his children and abdicate it to his wife. He needs to engage and be a vital part of the family life.

In fact, the Bible teaches that a man should not be considered for church leadership unless his home is in order. The scriptural emphasis is on him being an integral part of his family and leading them.

I once heard a man I respect share how he counseled a young pastor. The pastor naturally wanted his church and his ministry to grow and was frustrated it was not growing as he desired. This older man told him he should seek the Lord daily and try to make his wife and children feel loved and valued. He should lead in his home and love his wife so she would have a radiant countenance.

He shared with the younger pastor that if he sought God, tried to please Him in all he did, and loved his family and put them first, he would grow and so would his ministry. God would bless what he did. The young pastor wanted him to share programs, outreach efforts, and "secrets" to causing a church to grow. The older man emphasized his personal life, his relationship with God, and his family.

First Timothy 3 lists qualities a man should have before being considered for the office of an elder or church leader. The list includes, *"one who rules [leads] his own house well, having his children in submission with all reverence, (for if a man does not know how to rule his own house, how will he take care of the church of God?)"* (verses 4-5, NKJV). These qualifications are repeated in verse 12 when speaking of deacons in the church.

A similar qualification is given in Titus 1:6: *"If a man is blameless, the husband of one wife, having faithful children not accused of dissipation or insubordination."*

Clearly, a father is to lead his children in the ways of proper conduct, and teach them to respect and obey authority. This is a ministry every married man with children has—and an important one!

Next, let's look at another important topic; disciplining our children. Scores of books have been written about this topic. We will touch on some of the basic and important areas: disciplining our children, guiding their activities, and praying with them.

Disciplining Your Children

A father is supposed to discipline his children. For purposes of this study, let's define discipline as instruction and correction. Proper discipline is part of the process of teaching them, training them, and instilling godly character in them. *"Train up a child in the way he should go,"* Proverbs 22:6 says, *"and when he is old he will not depart from it."*

Discipline is a part of life—although not a part any of us enjoy. Proverbs 3:11-12 says, *"My son, do not despise the discipline of the LORD, nor detest His correction; for whom the LORD loves He corrects, just as a father the son in whom he delights."*

Those who will not accept discipline (instruction and correction) are headed for trouble because they are not willing to learn. We discipline, when needed, to reinforce the types of behavior that are acceptable and not acceptable. Our children need to know what is right and wrong, what is better and best, and what is God's standard. This is part of our job as parents.

The purpose of all discipline is to teach and train our children to have sound character and live their lives in a manner pleasing to God.

We are not perfect, our children are not perfect, and God does not expect us to be perfect. The goal of discipline is not to make us perfect, but to develop Christlike or biblical character. The same is true of our children. When we discipline them, it is not to make them perfect, but to help them to grow into people who have biblical values and seek God. They will make mistakes just as we have. Hopefully they will learn from those mistakes and become wiser.

Leading and teaching our children is not an impossible task or God would not have given it to us. As we go through life, we teach and instruct our children and take time to discuss the things they need to be taught. As we are doing this, God's Spirit is helping us as His truth is being shared.

The manner for discipline. One critical component is that all discipline must be done in love, not anger. James 1:20 says, *"The anger of man does not produce the righteousness of God."*

Being angry with our children does not cause them to be the children they need to be. An angry parent is a wounding parent. A loving parent is a nurturing parent. A parent who is firm when needed teaches boundaries that protect our children.

Anger breeds fear and, in turn, produces hurt and anger in our children. However, disciplining in love causes our children to know we love them and makes them feel secure in their relationships with us.

The strategy for discipline. It is important that parents have a discipline strategy to follow. A simple strategy might be:

Stage 1: Teach and instruct.
Stage 2: Remind and re-instruct.
Stage 3: Confront, re-teach, and warn of discipline.
Stage 4: Discipline. We must determine our children's motivation and respond accordingly.
- Rebellion and obvious disregard of instruction require immediate discipline.
- Negligence may call for a milder form of discipline.
- Forgetfulness calls for a yet milder form of discipline.

Stage 5: After the discipline, affirm the child with love. This means to restore the child by assuring them of your love and their importance to you. Discipline should not break relationship. Loving your children after discipline restores them, reassures them and keeps relationship strong.

This strategy starts with teaching appropriate behavior and then reinforces that teaching. "Discipline" itself happens only after the first stages, rather than out of irritation or anger in the moment.

Keys to Discipline. As you discipline your children, there are several keys to keep in mind. It should be:

1. Effective. Since the goal of all discipline is to teach and train our children, we must learn what type of discipline is most effective with our children. Discipline can consist of correcting them verbally, taking away privileges, sending them to their room for a time out, or other forms of discipline that might be effective.

There are many forms of discipline. It is beyond the scope of this work to identify and recommend which methods should be used, but I will say that, after disciplining your child, always affirm your love and restore him or her. Make it a time of instruction and reaffirmation of love. I realize many parents feel it is wrong to spank their children. But at times it can be necessary. Proverbs 13:24 says, *"He who spares the rod hates his son, but he who loves him is careful to discipline him."* The Living Bible says in the same verse, *"If you refuse to discipline your son, it proves you don't love him: for if you love him you will be prompt to punish him."*

The Bible is not teaching us to enjoy disciplining our children by spanking them. A loving parent never enjoys doing that. What it is saying is that if we love our children, we will discipline them when needed. Discipline is a part of teaching and training your children.

Sparing the rod teaches of not dealing with situations when needed, which can include spanking them by using something appropriate. Spanking is not beating and doing harm. It is getting the attention of the children and teaching them you are serious and what you are trying to teach them is serious. I am not speaking about child abuse or beating children. I am speaking of loving discipline that is necessary for the child. The whole point is to teach and instruct and after discipline to affirm your love and commitment to them.

Some children respond to parents without spanking and are sensitive to right and wrong. Obviously, if your children do not need it, then don't do it. If they will respond to other forms of discipline, then that is best. Each child is different and will respond differently to various types of discipline. Children will also often need a different type of discipline as they grow older.

Embarrassing our children, calling them names, yelling at them, or demeaning them are not effective or appropriate. These actions will wound them, rob them of self-confidence, and produce feelings of shame and rejection. They will weaken them, and our relationship with them, not strengthen them.

Parents should never discipline their children because they are an inconvenience or embarrassment. Focus on the children's need and what they need to learn. Fathers, you can be firm and let them know who's in charge without screaming. Yelling, screaming, and threatening without following through will cause frustration and wound both parties. Children will learn to wait it out and go about their way.

2. Unified. It is also critical that parents back each other up and show a unified front with the children. Children easily learn to play one parent against the other. If there is disagreement, discuss it together, come up with the needed discipline and carry it out. If parents have a strategy and carry it out, they can easily back each other up and be unified in discipline.

When our children were growing up, often Joan and I were not together on disciplining. I was the enforcer. She was kinder, patient, and more forgiving. As time passed, I came to realize that we needed input from each other and needed to be together in this. I wish I had realized that earlier. I must admit I was a more driven person who wanted immediate results. Joan was more patient. Together, we were a more "whole" person.

3. Early. It is important to start the discipline process when our children are young. As our children learn that when we expect obedience when we give instruction, and that we will follow through with discipline, they will respond by wanting to please loving parents and by wanting to avoid imminent discipline if they choose disobedience. If this is taught early, it normally will make our children more responsive to discipline and less in need of stronger discipline.

However, some children are strong-willed and may need consistent and frequent discipline for a period to establish obedience and responsiveness.

4. Firm. A parent does need to be firm when needed and follow through on discipline. If children learn that we will get upset, yell, and then later relent, that is not effective discipline. They will learn to wait out the process and then get their way. Remember, discipline is to teach and train, and it is to be done in love.

Your children must know you mean what you say and that you are committed to follow through with the process. This can be done in a firm but loving and consistent manner.

If your children are older, and you have neglected disciplining them and now have a mess on your hands, it probably won't be easy—but it can be done. You must talk to them—maybe even apologize for your lack of discipline and admit to not being the parent they need. Then you must establish the rules, affirm your love motivation, and move forward. As you do this, continue to communicate, affirm your love motivation, and continue to be firm.

For Further Study

Here are additional scriptures you can study about discipline:

Foolishness is bound up in the heart of a child, but the rod of correction will drive it far from him. (Proverbs 22:15)

The rod and reproof give wisdom, but a child left to himself brings shame to his mother. (Proverbs 29:15)

A wise son heeds his father's instruction, but a scoffer does not listen to rebuke. (Proverbs 13:1)

He who spares his rod hates his son, but he who loves him disciplines him promptly. (Proverbs 13:24)

A fool despises his father's instruction, but he who receives reproof is prudent. (Proverbs 15:5)

Guiding Activities

Another aspect of leading our children is to oversee their activities. Fathers, do not let your children be involved in questionable or unscriptural activities. We must not give in to the customs and philosophies of the world's culture when they are contrary to the Bible. Allowing our children to do things because others are doing them is a grave mistake.

We are to know the difference between the *"unclean and clean, the holy and unholy"* (Leviticus 10:10-11), and we must teach these differences to our children. Ezekiel 44:23 says Israel's priests *"shall teach My people the difference between the holy and the unholy, and cause them to discern between the unclean and the clean"* (Ezekiel 44:23).

These verses refer to the priests who were to teach their people. However, all men are called to be priests and teachers in their homes. They are to teach their children the difference between right and wrong—what is pleasing to God and what is not. God desires His people to have clean hands and hearts:

> *Who may ascend into the hill [presence] of the LORD? He who has clean hands and a pure heart, who has not lifted up his soul to an idol. (Psalm 24:3-5)*

Obviously, our hands and heart cannot be clean if we are participating in things that are wrong or sinful. We must study God's Word to know those things that are right in God's sight, and those that are not. We are also to teach these things to our children so that they will know how to conduct themselves in a manner that is pleasing to the Lord. We are to protect our children by being resolute not to allow them to be involved in inappropriate activities.

Most important, we must not merely teach our children the "dos and don'ts," we must also talk to them about God's love and the priority of seeking and knowing Him. Our job is to teach them there is a reward for doing right and a consequence for doing wrong.

Praying with Your Children

As we lead our children in God's ways, it is key that we teach them about prayer and that we pray with them. It is amazing that many seminaries do not teach their prospective ministry students about prayer. Prayer is one of the keys to our spiritual walk with God. Most churches do not even teach about this. Perhaps it is because the pastor was not taught about the importance of prayer.

However, Jesus practiced and modeled prayer. He spent whole nights in prayer. To Him prayer, which was time with His Father, was essential. Jesus taught His disciples to pray (Matthew 6:5-15). He also taught us that we should persist in prayer (Luke 19:1-8). Likewise, we should encourage our children to pray and pray with them.

While a repetitive prayer each night is good, it will not teach children how to pray. We need to show them how to pray about their lives and their needs, teaching them to seek God and ask God to reveal His truth to them.

As our children get older, we need to teach them how to seek God regarding the important areas of life. Their future mate, their work and career, their values, and their activities are all critical decisions; they need to seek God for direction in all areas of their lives.

We also need to persist in praying for our children. Some areas in which to pray for our children are:

- their salvation
- their relationship with God

- their hearts and attitudes
- their problem areas
- insight and wisdom for you and them
- their choice of friends
- their education
- their work, life, and career
- their future mate
- for their protection physically and spiritually
- everything in general that concerns them

We pray over these areas as we need to and as God's Spirit leads us to. As a father prays for his children, he should ask God to intervene and be active in their lives. Influencing and teaching our children their need to have relationship with their heavenly Father is vital to their lives. We can't make them. But we can lead them and teach them.

As we spend daily time with God, we can teach them the importance for them to have daily time with God. Daily prayer and Bible study are the foundation to learning about God and knowing His truth. Praying for our children that they will develop a hunger and thirst for God and His truth is a great way to pray for them.

As fathers, we must not allow the world or the enemy to claim our children. We should take the leadership to be loving, vigilant, and protective. It is our God-given responsibility as fathers to teach them the ways of the Lord and His love for them as we discipline and guide them.

I fully realize we can't force our children to accept Christ and follow Him. However, the Bible tells us to teach our children about God and His ways. When we do this, we plant seeds that the Holy Spirit uses in our children's lives. They will not forget our example and our loving instruction.

QUESTIONS FOR REFLECTION AND DISCUSSION

1. What is your goal in disciplining your children?

2. Have you discussed discipline with your wife and agreed upon a discipline strategy or practice? If so, what is it? Are you united in this strategy?

3. Generally, do you discipline your children with an undertone of love, or of anger?

4. Do you watch over your children and keep aware of their activities? How do you do this?

5. Do you pray regularly with your children? If not, are you willing to begin to do this regularly?

_____

_____

_____

TAKE A KNEE

Let's pray: *"Father, I want to discipline my children with love and kindness. I want to learn to be both firm and loving as the situation needs. I also want to pray with my children and teach them to pray and seek You about their lives. I commit these areas to You and again ask for Your leadership, wisdom, and insight in these areas."*

Chapter 5

Passing on Godly Character

"Another thing you do: You flood the Lord's altar with tears. You weep and wail because He no longer pays attention to your offerings or accepts them with pleasure from your hands. You ask, 'Why?'. It is because the Lord is acting as the witness between you and the wife of your youth, because you have broken faith with her, though she is your partner, the wife of your marriage covenant. Has not the Lord made them one? In flesh and spirit they are His. And why one? Because He was seeking godly offspring. So guard yourself in your spirit, and do not break faith with the wife of your youth." (Malachi 2:13-15, NIV)

The above scripture states that God desires godly offspring. It also stresses that God desires a man to be faithful to his wife and not neglect her. But the emphasis of this book is on children. (Another book in this series, *A Man and His Wife*, is devoted to a man's relationship with his wife). Godly parenting means we are to strive to raise up, or grow up, children with godly character. By the way, godly characteristics are all through the Bible. Honesty, integrity, work ethic, compassion, kindness, and thriftiness are some godly characteristics. As you study the Bible you will see more. The book of Proverbs is full of godly characteristics.

So, what is godly or biblical character, and how do we achieve it? *Webster's Dictionary* defines character as "the particular qualities, impressed by nature or habit on a person, which distinguishes him from others." Our character is who we are and how we behave ourselves. It is our values, our convictions, our actions and beliefs. We are to grow in character, and also teach our children how to grow in it.

Character Starts with Us

Growing as a man and a father is a challenge. As we seek God, we will be stretched and changed as we grow. The question is, are we willing to be stretched? Are we willing to allow God to change us where needed? Are we willing to spend time in the Bible, studying it to learn how we are to live? Are we willing to spend daily time in prayer over our lives and ask God to change us and reveal His truth to us? If we are, our character will change, and the heritage we pass along to our children will change as well.

As a young man, others challenged me to grow and change in these ways. Plus, I was often put into situations where I had to learn and grow. Painfully at times, my shortcomings were pointed out to me and I had a choice: pray and ask God to change me or keep going as I was. None of us are perfect and we all need to grow and allow God to change us. We will never be perfect in this life.

PASSING ON GODLY CHARACTER

But we can submit to the Lord and allow Him to grow us, change us, and love us.

Developing godly or biblical character should be every father's goal. We need an open heart and allow the Holy Spirit to do His work in our lives. Better yet, invite the Holy Spirit to do His work. If we truly want to grow, we will. If we truly want God's Spirit to do His work in us, He will. Resist or submit; be open or closed; chose to humble ourselves or be stubborn and prideful—those choices are the key to growing as we respond to God's Spirit and His Word.

The Bible teaches us what godly character is. It teaches us what we are to believe, how we are to behave, and the principles by which we are to live. For example, the following verse gives clear instruction to fathers: *"But if anyone does not provide for his own, and especially for those of his household, he has denied the faith and is worse than an unbeliever"* (1 Timothy 5:8). From this and other scriptures, we learn that we are to work and provide for our families. The Bible also teaches us to be honest and fair in all of our dealings. Again, these are godly or biblical character traits that we are to practice.

As we read the Bible, we learn these traits and values. As we read the Bible and see how God wants us to live, we should pray and ask God to make these qualities real in our lives. Beyond that, we need to choose to practice these things in our lives. The Bible promises that if we live according to God's truth, we will be blessed.

> *Blessed is the man who walks not in the counsel of the ungodly, nor stands in the path of sinners, not sits in the seat of the scornful; but his delight is in the law of the LORD, and in His law he meditates day and night. He shall be like a tree planted by the rivers of water, that brings forth its fruit*

in its season, whose leaf also shall not wither; and whatever he does shall prosper. (Psalm 1:1-4)

What great promises from God!

Joseph was a man who sought after God and tried to please Him in all he did. He found himself in prison, wrongfully accused of an act he did not commit. Where was God in this? Was this his reward for trying to please Him? However, Joseph continued to believe and trust in God. During the years in prison, God was developing character in Joseph, character he needed to fulfill God's plan for his life. He went from being a favored son of a wealthy man with servants to a slave and convict, through no fault of his own. He was a slave and convict for thirteen years when suddenly it changed.

Why did it take thirteen years? What all was God doing in his life? We don't have all of these answers. But we do know that God fulfilled all of His promises to Joseph and prepared him for a highly significant position.

At the proper time, not only was Joseph released, he was also elevated to an unbelievable position as governor of the entire land of Egypt. God prepared Joseph for His plan for his life by developing his character, and because of it Joseph experienced God's blessings (Genesis chapters 37-42).

In the same way, we must allow God to develop His character in us, so that we can develop His traits in us, and in turn in our children. Remember, what your children see in your life will outshine what you teach them. They need to be taught and trained, but they will also watch your example.

God teaches and trains us in the little things, so we can handle the big things.

Fruits of the Spirit

Galatians 5 speaks of "fruit" in our lives. This fruit is a natural outworking of God's Spirit in us. When we accepted Christ, God's Spirit took up residence in us and desires to release His "fruit" in us.

In Him you also trusted, after you heard the word of truth, the gospel of your salvation; in whom also, having believed, you were sealed with the Holy Spirit of promise, who is the guarantee of our inheritance until the redemption of the purchase possession, to the praise of His glory. (Ephesians 1:13-14)

God's Spirit wants to release in us, and through us, the fruit mentioned in Galatians 5: "love, joy, peace, patience, kindness, faithfulness, gentleness, self-control."

It is interesting that, in this passage, the Bible does not speak of talents or abilities. While those are God-given, the emphasis here is on our character and attitudes toward others. God is more interested in how we treat others than in our accomplishments in life.

Regardless of our talents or abilities, God wants His "fruit" to be part of our character, our nature. Christ, while on earth, had these qualities flowing out of Him. God's Spirit wants to reproduce Christ's life, character, and nature in us.

God is more concerned about our character, than our talents and abilities

When we are yielded to God's Spirit, these qualities will flow out of us. Conversely, a pattern of anger, a lack of patience, a lack of joy, having an unkind nature, lacking self-control, all show a lack of God's Spirit being released in our lives. All Christians have God's Spirit in them, but He may be hindered from flowing out of us by our unwillingness or the condition of our hearts.

Think of there being barriers in our hearts that block the flow of God's Spirit. God wants to remove the barriers so there can be more of a free flowing of His Spirit through us. This happens as our mind is renewed. Our thinking changes and comes into agreement with God and His truth. This "transforms" us and changes our life. Our mind is renewed by realizing the truth and accepting it in our life. This happens by taking in the Word or truth of God. That's why we must study God's Word: to be transformed and renewed.

> *"Do not conform any longer to the pattern of this world, but be transformed by the renewing of your mind. Then you will be able to test and approve what God's will is—His good, pleasing and perfect will." (Romans 12:2)*

To the extent we spend time in God's Word, we will become renewed in our thinking. We will think differently and live differently. We will see God's activity increase in our life, His power released in us more often and in greater ways. We will become vessels God can and will use more.

Want to see more of God's activity in your life? Spend more time with Him, and let Him renew you.

The good news is that God desires to change us so the fruit of His Spirit does flow in us and through us. This is a good thing! And when we experience God's Spirit changing our character to be like Christ, we are also able to begin to help our children develop these character qualities.

Patience and Kindness

Just as we are not perfect and need God to be patient with us, our children are not perfect and need us to be patient with them. Patience does not mean we do not deal with areas and behaviors that need to be corrected. However, it does mean we do it in patience, because we love our children. The Bible says, *"Love is patient, love is kind"* (1 Corinthians 13:4).

Children whose fathers are perfectionists, angry, or overdemanding are likely to develop negative behaviors. They may feel inferior and think they can never measure up, and they will hunger for love, acceptance, kindness, understanding, and forgiveness.

Colossians 3:21 instructs, *"Fathers, do not provoke [exasperate] your children, lest they become discouraged."* The word used in this passage, *provoke* or *exasperate*, means either to stir up to anger or to stir up by anger. We can discourage or wound our children by being an angry father. We can breed anger into our children as a reaction to our anger toward them. Ephesians 6:4 repeats, *"And you fathers, do not provoke your children to wrath, but bring them up in the training and admonition of the Lord."*

Children long for relationship with their fathers. Yes, they need to be trained, taught, disciplined, and corrected. But more important, they need to be loved and shown kindness and patience. A child who is shown no patience will most likely show little to others, or he might retreat to avoid conflict.

If you as a father struggle with patience and anger, stop now and pray. You must realize it is sin and harmful to your life and to your wife and children. If you struggle in the areas of showing kindness and patience, you need to pray and ask God to change you. Ask Him to change your heart and reproduce the fruit of His Spirit in you. He will.

Many men see qualities such as patience and kindness as weakness. This is not only untrue and unscriptural, it is a deception and part of the thinking of the world system. It is an "antichrist" mentality. We can be gentle and patient, yet courageous, bold, and firm. The difference is our motivation.

Boldness and Courage

When the situation calls for it, we are to be bold and courageous. *"The wicked flee when no one pursues, but the righteous are bold as a lion"* (Proverbs 28:1).

God wants us to have character with courage and boldness. God told Joshua, *"Be strong and of good courage; do not be afraid, nor be dismayed, for the LORD your God is with you wherever you go"* (Joshua 1:9).

God's admonition to Joshua was for him to choose to be strong and courageous in order to fulfill the tasks God had for him. He could do this because God was with him.

Obviously, God wants men to display the character traits of boldness and courage, as well as those of patience and kindness. The problem is that the world has warped the concepts of these qualities.

Meekness, humility, compassion, patience, and kindness are also godly qualities. We are not cowards or lacking in courage when the situation calls for meekness or humility. A man practices love and humility not out of fear, but because it is Christlike and manly.

Just so, a man practices courage and boldness because it is Christlike and manly. Teaching this to your children and helping them to understand this will have enormous value in their lives.

Here's a challenge for you: I encourage you to do a word study on the following words: meekness, humility, compassion, patience, kindness, courage, and boldness. Look these words up in the dictionary and then in a Bible concordance that gives the meaning of the Greek and Hebrew words. (Two free websites that give Greek and Hebrew meanings are BibleGateway.com and StudyLight.org; these are great reference tools.)

Fathers should not allow their children to grow up afraid of others. This is especially important for boys. Young boys who grow up fearful and afraid are handicapped in life. Proverbs 29:25 states, *"The fear of man brings a snare, but whoever trusts in the Lord shall be safe."*

Fathers need to teach their sons courage and boldness. Young boys should not live in fear of bullies or be afraid to stick up for themselves when it is appropriate. Just as husbands must be willing to defend their wives, a boy or young man should be taught this principle of self-defense and defending others.

The Israelite men were taught war and became skilled warriors in order to defend their nation and families. This did not mean they were not loving and kind with their families. It also does not mean they bullied or were mean-spirited toward others. It does mean they were courageous and bold when needed. Jesus was kind, gentle, and compassionate to all who came to Him. But He also spoke and demonstrated the truth as it was needed.

Boys must learn to display courage and be ready to defend themselves or others when necessary. This doesn't mean a boy is to be an angry person, but a courageous one. He can be taught to be both a peacemaker, when appropriate, and to have courage and boldness, when appropriate.

Jesus was a great example. He was gentle, loving, and forgiving. But He was also bold and reproved the hypocritical religious leaders by calling them hypocrites (Matthew 15:1-7). He physically drove out the money changers from the temple and overturned their tables (Matthew 21:12-13). Jesus showed great courage when needed, and tenderness and concern when it was needed.

Daughters should also be taught to be courageous and have courage to stand up for what is right. Young girls who grow up fearful and afraid are also handicapped for life. A fearful girl without boldness or courage or the ability to take a stand is in a fairly desperate place when she hits junior high and high school and faces intense peer pressure, social media bullying, cliques, and intense sexual pressure to conform and compromise.

Our sons and daughters need to be mighty in spirit. They need the ability to show love and compassion, and also to show courage and be bold when needed. They need to know how to stick up for themselves when appropriate and not be afraid of mean-spirited people. They may not fight with a physical sword, but can fight with the sword of the Spirit, the truth of God. A girl can be gentle and loving, and still be courageous and bold when needed. Being a girl doesn't mean she does not have courage and cannot take a stand. She should be taught to be courageous when needed and stand up for what is right.

Courage is not just being willing to fight physically if necessary, but being willing to take a stand when needed. Courage is standing for what is right, and our children should be taught to do so.

Godly Character

It is important that you and your children realize that the development of biblical character is a high priority. Part of being a Christian is learning to cooperate with God's working in you through His Spirit, and seek Him for understanding of His purposes and plans for you. In addition, your children need to know this.

Seek God for understanding of what He desires for your life. He will reveal it to you. Embrace this process and trust God for the outcome. The Christian life was not meant to be dull!

QUESTIONS FOR REFLECTION AND DISCUSSION

1. Of the fruit of the Spirit—love, joy, peace, patience, kindness, goodness, faithfulness, gentleness, self-control—are

there any qualities in which you would particularly like to grow as a father?

_____

_____

2. If you have children, list their names below. Then, beside each one, list an area or situation in which they particularly need patience and kindness from you (these may be the areas in which you find patience most difficult or where they are especially vulnerable or needy). Also list areas where you need to be firm instead of giving in, for the sake of your children.

_____

_____

3. How can you be deliberate in showing patience and kindness when needed?

_____

_____

4. How can you be more firm when needed?

_____

_____

5. Do you teach your children boldness and courage as well as compassion and kindness? How do you do this?

_____

_____

TAKE A KNEE

Let's pray: *"Lord, develop in me the character you desire. Teach me to be both bold and courageous when needed, as well as to be humble and mild when needed. I want to be the man You desire me to be, complete with Christlike character. I know this is a lifelong process, so begin Your work in me now. I ask You do to do so, knowing I can trust You and that You only have good for me. Thank You that You love and care for me."*

A FINAL WORD

It has always been God's desire for children and their fathers to have a close, meaningful relationship. God gives us a great promise in Malachi 4:5-6:

> *Behold, I will send you Elijah the prophet before the coming of the great and dreadful day of the LORD. And he will turn the hearts of the fathers to the children, and the hearts of the children to their fathers, lest I come and strike the earth with a curse.*

God promises that prior to His great judgment on mankind in the end times, He will send a prophetic message to restore the relationship of fathers with their children. He states that this must happen to avert a curse coming on the earth. This verse shows the importance of a father's relationship with his children and his role in teaching, training, and loving them. Is it any wonder that divorce and absent fathers are bringing confusion and lack of true direction to their children as fathers are separated from their children? A father can never minimize his role in his children's lives.

The enemy, Satan, and his forces are always trying to destroy families. In particular, they are trying to tear down fatherhood and manhood. In today's society, men are made fun of just because they are men. They are portrayed on TV as foolish, unwise, and being out of touch with reality.

A FINAL WORD

God desires to raise up a generation of godly fathers who, in turn, will reproduce godly families, *"lest I come and strike the earth with a curse"* (Malachi 4:6) If the enemy is successful in destroying families, the people of the earth will feel its effects. As men, let us seek the Lord and stand in the gap for our families. Let us stand strong, be vigilant, not fall prey to the enemy, nor allow our families to do so.

"Be on your guard; stand firm in the faith;
be men of courage; be strong. Do everything in love."
(1 Corinthians 16:13-14)

ABOUT THE AUTHOR

Lou Turner wrote *Living Life God's Way* out of his passion for men to discover God, and to get to know Him and what He has for them. This 13-book men's discipleship series is the culmination of Lou's own journey—a life of seeking God, studying His Word, memorizing Scripture and meditating on it, and practical experience with family, community, marketplace work, and Christian ministry. It also comes, by Lou's own admission, from life experiences of both successes and mistakes, as a result of both good and bad decisions.

Lou has headed ministries, written and taught workshops, classes, and seminars, and discipled dozens of men. Now, he has put into print the things he has learned to help other men along their path and journey.

Most of Lou's growing up years were spent in Detroit and its suburbs, where he was raised in a pastor's home. Following his graduation from university with a Bachelor of Science in Business Administration, Lou and his wife planted and pastored a church for three years. After that time, he felt the strong call of God to return to business.

Over the years, Lou has served in numerous senior executive positions with national and international companies in the real estate and oil and gas industries. As of this writing, Lou is still active in business with his own home building company. He has

ABOUT THE AUTHOR

been married to his wife Joan since they were 20. They have three children and 10 grandchildren and make their home in Phoenix, Arizona.

www.ingramcontent.com/pod-product-compliance
Lightning Source LLC
Chambersburg PA
CBHW021121080526
44587CB00010B/598